MW01040958

BABY NAME

....

F

N

HIGH CONTRAST + CLEAR SHAPES = BABY

APPLE

BALLOON

CAT

DOG

EGG

FLOWER

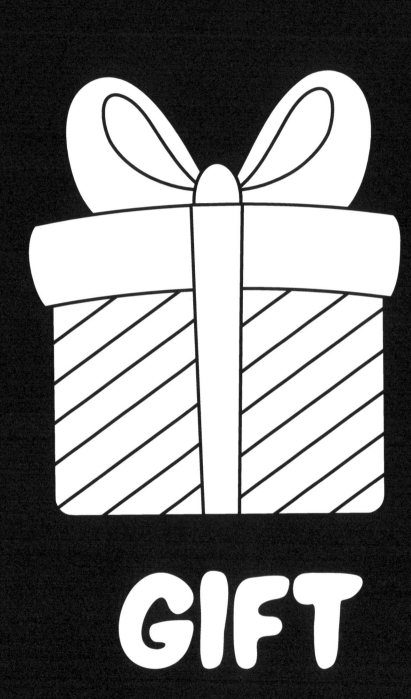

GIFT

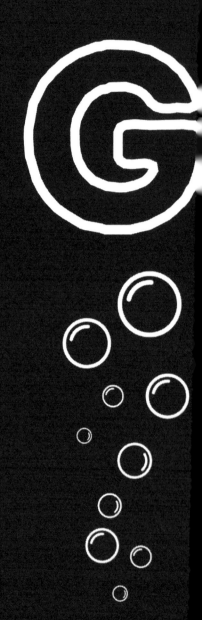

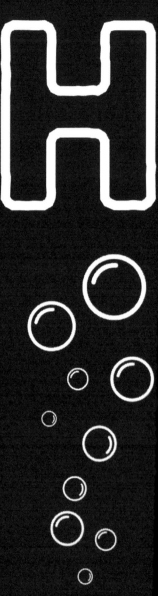

HAT

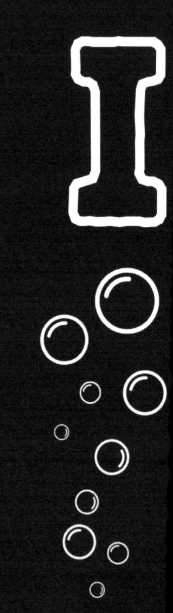

ICE CREAM

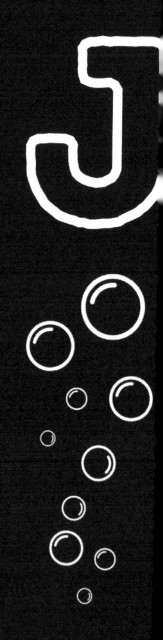

JUICE

KANGAROO

LAMB

MOON

NEST

OWL

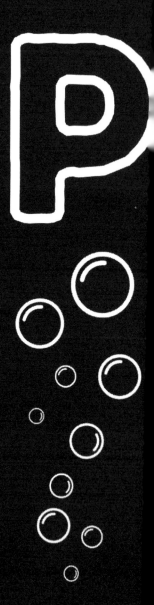

PIE

QUILT

RAINBOW

R

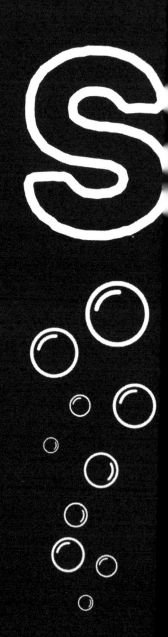

SUN

TREE

UMBRELLA

VASE

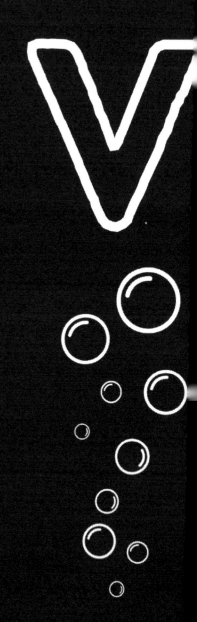

WORM

X

XYLOPHONE

YOGURT

ZEBRA

Thank You

Thank you for your purchase, If you have a moment to spare, please leave us a review, we would be really grateful and very happy to read it

Made in the USA
Las Vegas, NV
12 October 2023

78997116R00033